THE TREE

Created by Gallimard Jeunesse
and Pascale de Bourgoing
Illustrated by Christian Broutin

A FIRST DISCOVERY BOOK

Cartwheel
·B·O·O·K·S· ™

SCHOLASTIC INC.
New York   Toronto   London   Auckland   Sydney

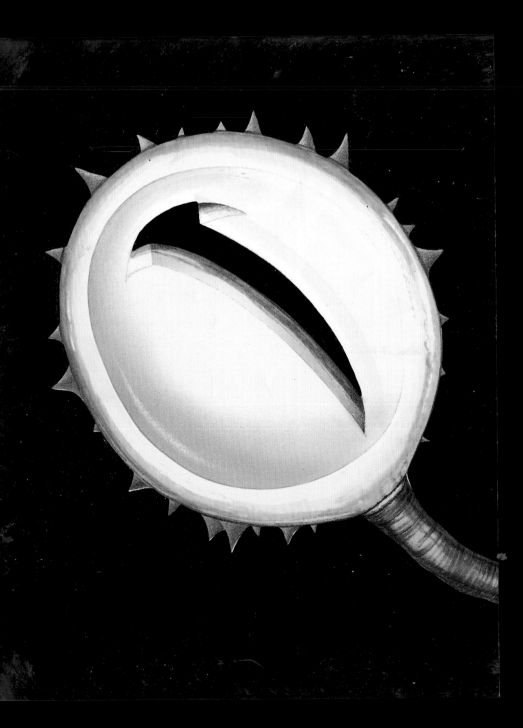

There's a shiny brown chestnut
inside the green burr.

What is hidden inside this green
and prickly covering?

A chestnut is the seed
of a chestnut tree.
A tree is a giant plant.
Food stored inside the seed
nourishes the young plant.
As the chestnut sapling grows up,
the roots grow down into the soil.

The mature tree's roots
push down deep into the earth.
They drink up water from the soil.

By winter's end, the
chestnut tree has
thousands of tiny buds.
When spring comes and
it is warm again,
the buds will bloom.

The buds
burst open,
revealing many
tiny leaves.

In spring,
the chestnut tree
blossoms.

Little by little,
flowers become
chestnuts.

In the heat
of summer,
the chestnuts
grow large
and ripen.

In early
autumn, the
chestnuts begin
to fall.

See how the leaves
on the trees have
changed to bright
orange, yellow,
and gold!

Winter is coming. The leaves start to fall.

Many animals and insects make
homes in and around trees.
Trees provide food and shelter.
Let's see who lives in this tree.

You can learn
to recognize different
kinds of trees by their
sizes and their shapes.

The beech
is very big.

In autumn, the maple
is round and golden.

The poplar
is tall and pointy.

The weeping willow's
branches droop and bend.

The birch is thin,
with white bark.

You can also learn to recognize trees by the shape of their leaves and the look of their seeds.

| The American chestnut's leaf has tiny teeth along its edges. | The leaf of the hazel tree is shaped like a heart. | The oak tree's leaf has rounded edges. |

Chestnut

Hazelnut

Acorn

The walnut tree's
leaf is made up
of many small leaves.

The maple leaf
has five points.

Walnut

Maple seed

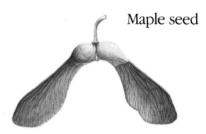

The pine tree
and its cousins
stay green
all year-round.
They are called
evergreens.

Cypress

Sequoia

Fir

Their fruits are cones that enclose the seeds.

Their leaves
are sharp and
do not fall
in autumn.
We call the leaves needles.

Cedar   Parasol pine

We make many things from the wood
we get from trees.

Paper is made from wood.
With paper, we can make a book . . . about trees!

Trees are the oldest living things on earth.
They give us food and medicine.
They produce the oxygen that we breathe.
Trees make our lives better in hundreds of ways.
We should try to conserve trees.
You can help by recycling paper.
Or plant a tree and watch it grow!

Titles in the series of *First Discovery Books*:

Airplanes	**The Earth and Sky**
and Flying Machines	**The Egg**
Bears	**Flowers**
Birds	**Fruit**
Castles	**The Ladybug**
Cats	**and Other Insects**
Colors	**The Tree**
Dinosaurs	**Weather**

Copyright © 1989 by Editions Gallimard.
Originally published in France under the title *L'arbre* by Editions Gallimard.

This edition English translation by Karen Backstein.
This edition American text by Louise Goldsen.
All rights reserved. First published in the U.S.A. in 1992
by Scholastic Inc., by arrangement with Editions Gallimard.
CARTWHEEL BOOKS is a trademark of Scholastic Inc.

Library of Congress Cataloging-in-Publication Data

Bourgoing, Pascale de.
    [Arbre. English]
    The Tree/created by Gallimard Jeunesse and Pascale de Bourgoing;
    illustrated by Christian Broutin.
        p.   cm. — (A first discovery book)
    Translation of: L'arbre.
    Summary: Follows a chestnut tree through the seasons as it sprouts from its seed, blossoms, grows, sheds leaves, and drops new chestnuts that will one day become trees, too. Includes a description of different types of trees and how to recognize them.

    ISBN 0-590-45265-7

    1. Trees — Juvenile literature. [1. Trees.]   I. Christian Broutin, ill.
II. Gallimard Jeunesse.   III. Title.   IV. Series.
QK475.8.B6913   1992
582.16 — dc20

                                                                            91-25938
                                                                            CIP
                                                                            AC

12 11 10 9 8 7 6 5

2 3 4 5 6 7/9

Printed in Italy by Editoriale Libraria

First Scholastic printing, March 1992